CSU Poetry Series XXXVII

Poems by Jared Carter

Jared Carter

After the Rain

Jared Carter

Cleveland State University
Poetry Center

Acknowledgments appear on page 101.

Quoted portions of parts 1 and 2 of "This Is Not a Poem" are from "American Victims of Hiroshima" by Robert Karl Manoff, which first appeared in *The New York Times Magazine*. Copyright © 1984 by The New York Times Company. Reprinted by permission.

Manufactured in the United States of America

ISBN 1-880834-03-0 (cloth)
    0-914946-97-8 (paper)

Library of Congress Catalog Card Number: 92-70728

Second printing, November 1993.

Funded Through
Ohio Arts Council

727 East Main Street
Columbus, Ohio 43205-1796
(614) 466-2613

Contents

Six

Acknowledgments

for Diane
Heart in bond, spirit free

After the Rain

After the rain, it's time to walk the field
again, near where the river bends. Each year
I come to look for what this place will yield—
lost things still rising here.

The farmer's plow turns over, without fail,
a crop of arrowheads, but where or why
they fall is hard to say. They seem, like hail,
dropped from an empty sky,

yet for an hour or two, after the rain
has washed away the dusty afterbirth
of their return, a few will show up plain
on the reopened earth.

Still, even these are hard to see—
at first they look like any other stone.
The trick to finding them is not to be
too sure about what's known;

conviction's liable to say straight off
this one's a leaf, or that one's merely clay,
and miss the point: after the rain, soft
furrows show one way

across the field, but what is hidden here
requires a different view—the glance of one
not looking straight ahead, who in the clear
light of the morning sun

simply keeps wandering across the rows,
letting his own perspective change.
After the rain, perhaps, something will show,
glittering and strange.

One

Phoenix

Right from Merom on State Road 63 to the junction
with the Mann Cemetery Road . . . left here across
the prairie to other Mounds, also under cultivation,
and to Mann Cemetery. . . .

Here are buried two of General Harrison's soldiers,
Kentuckians who carried an old family feud into the
army and killed each other on the way to the Battle of
Tippecanoe. . . .

At Graysville Road . . . right to a bridge over Big
Springs, branch of Turman Creek. Fifty yards left of
the bridge is the spring where General Harrison's
expeditionary army camped the night of September 29,
1811.

It was at this spring that the two soldiers from
Kentucky slew each other. The waters of the spring
are caught now in a moss-covered brick enclosure.

Indiana: A Guide to the Hoosier State

He knew. They all knew, there was no use
pretending. The Shawnees knew. We knew
they were out there. They knew we were
coming. Everybody knew. We all knew why.

Why didn't he and I fight and be done with it?
Why did we bother to join up, put on those coats
with the strange buttons, why did we drill
and march, side by side, but never speak?

The General knew, and we knew. That evening
when he sent the two of us down to the spring,
and told us to leave our rifles behind,
we understood. At the bottom of that hollow,

beneath a limestone ledge, a dark presence
rose up—a basin of troubled water, seething
and boiling, surging over heaps of stones,
catching the last light through the trees—

and after a while, when we had filled
all the canteens, one by one, both of us
kneeling there, reaching into the depths,
our fingers gone half numb—there were no

clear reflections, only the broken heave
of light and dark, and it seemed as though
that motion had found its way inside me,
and I knew we could put it off no longer.

We had come all this way, with the Shawnees
waiting for us. They were out there now,
watching. I couldn't risk their taking him;
somehow he belonged to me, and me to him.

I drew my skinning knife and looked across
and saw him crouched there with his dagger.
We stumbled through the shallows, smashing
against each other like a pair of rams.

His blade burned deep in my right side
but I knew the spring would cool the pain
and soon I would be free of an old anger,
the resentment I had carried for so long.

I shoved my knife clear to the hilt up
inside him, and stood for a moment lifting
with both hands, holding him on its point,
before he fell away, taking me with him,

out onto the pool. From where we landed,
tangled in each other's arms, neither of us
had the strength to move. We lay gasping;
dark plumes began to spread around us.

I could not feel the water's coldness.
I struggled, trying to push him away,
but he clung fast. I took a deep breath
and found I could still speak. I said

his name—it was my father's middle name,
and he stirred, as though hearing someone
calling from a long way off. His eyelids
fluttered, and I decided to talk to him,

to let him know I was still there. I tried
to make the sound of my own voice rise up
above the gurgle of the spring. I told him
he had my father's middle name. I recited

the names of my sisters, brothers, aunts,
uncles, my mother. I said my mother's name
again. There was no reply. He came closer,
his face half out of the troubled surface.

I told him the names of our hunting dogs,
and our horse, and the horse before that.
I told him I thought night would come soon.
Finally I began to tell him what Bob Petty,

the old schoolmaster, had explained to me
just the day before—about the creature
with outstretched wings, the bird stamped
on the ormolu buttons of our uniforms.

I told him what Petty had said: those coats
were originally designed for Napoleon,
for the soldiers in his army, for when
he finished with Europe, and got ready

to come over to America. Those uniforms
were stored in a warehouse somewhere
down in New Orleans. But then Napoleon
sold everything west of the Mississippi

to Tom Jefferson, and the uniforms got
left behind when the French pulled out.
General Harrison had heard about them,
and bought them cheap, for this campaign.

All that time, on the march from Vincennes,
we had touched these strange buttons, morning
and night, but never known. I went on talking,
there in the twilight, in case he was listening.

What can you do with a man who insists on
stealing away, while you cling to the edge
of an endless flow, but still have something
important to say? My voice was a whisper now.

The bird was called a phoenix—a creature
that would never die, that built its nest
in fire, and rose up from its own ashes.
It could sleep, Petty said, on the waves

of the sea, even in the midst of a storm.
I came to the end, but he no longer seemed
to care. This time, when he drifted off,
I let him go, out toward the deepest part.

A darkness had spread over the spring,
but I hung on to the moss and boulders
there at the edge, and by the last light
I watched the water all turn clear again.

Scryer

The first time when I was thirteen mother
came into my room that night saying there
there you've been dreaming it's only a bad

dream but I could still see a strange light
everywhere, horses banging against the stalls,
my father and brothers running, calling out

it's only a dream she said now go to sleep.
Next morning I told them but no one listened,
no one remembered three weeks later when

the barn burned to the ground though they
managed to save the horses. The second time
I was fourteen and told no one I had seen

a neighbor drifting face down in the river,
there there go to sleep it's only a dream.
I stood and wept the day they buried him

though no one knew why—stood praying
in the churchyard let there be no third time,
I could not bear to look into that stream again,

that dark shining, let no one hear or remember
what I dream in the night. But the preacher heard,
and knew I would not tell, and took me away,

down to the river. When he had finished
he gave me a ring with a crystal stone
and I looked in its heart and fell asleep

and knew it was not horses or men I saw into
but fire turned hard as ice, and brimming with light
and a voice in the night saying there there

The Gleaning

All day long they have been threshing
and something breaks: the canvas belt
that drives the separator flies off,
parts explode through the swirl
of smoke and chaff, and he is dead
where he stands—drops the pitchfork
as they turn to look at him—and falls.
They carry him to the house and go on
with the work. Five wagons and their teams
stand waiting, it is still daylight,
there will be time enough for grieving.

When the undertaker comes from town
he brings the barber, who must wait
till the women finish washing the body.
Neighbors arrive from the next farm
to take the children. The machines
shut down, one by one, horses
are led away, the air grows still
and empty, then begins to fill up
with the sounds of cicada and mourning dove.
The men stand along the porch, talking
in low voices, smoking their cigarettes;
the undertaker sits in the kitchen
with the family.
                    In the parlor
the barber throws back the curtains
and talks to this man, whom he has known
all his life, since they were boys
together. As he works up a lather
and brushes it onto his cheeks,
he tells him the latest joke. He strops
the razor, tests it against his thumb,
and scolds him for not being more careful.
Then with darkness coming over the room

he lights a lamp, and begins to scrape
at the curve of the throat, tilting the head
this way and that, stretching the skin,
flinging the soap into a basin, gradually
leaving the face glistening and smooth.

And as though his friend had fallen asleep
and it were time now for him to stand up
and stretch his arms, and look at his face
in the mirror, and feel the closeness
of the shave, and marvel at his dreaming—
the barber trims the lamp, and leans down,
and says, for a last time, his name.

The Shriving

And the seventh angel poured out his vial into the air.

Revelation 16:17

He was a druggist. The storefront building
had one long room with a pressed-tin ceiling,
a line of revolving fans down the middle,
and random-oak floors darkened with polishing.
The soda-fountain counter was a slab
of black glass chipped with tiny moons.
There were tables and chairs made of wire
where you brought your date after a game:
you could look up and see yourself in the mirror.
The boys who worked there had imported brooms
with handles maybe ten feet long or more;
once each week they had to sweep the ceiling.
When the brooms wore out, the druggist took them,
saved them for a time when he burnt the worms.

Save for the times when he burnt the worms,
I never saw him smile. If those who lived there
had a name for sacred, they never said it aloud.
Once when I was small the aunties took me out
to a grove of walnut trees with nothing else
around them, no green thing strong enough
to rise up from that ground. Some called it
poison, others spoke of a strange power
in the earth itself, which the tree could summon.
My morning there, gathering nuts—black
clinkers—stained my fingers for weeks after.
And from my first glimpse of that place I knew
there are some things not written in books,
there are some trees whose names you know on sight.

These are the names of the trees I came to know:
willow, which is first to turn green in springtime,
poplar, which looks silver when the wind blows,
oak, which is always last to let go of its leaves.

Each time he turned the car into the lane
he praised the walnut trees that stood there:
how they would bring a fortune at the mill,
how their heartwood, sliced thin as paper,
would unfold like ripples in a stream.
But they were his possession now, they came
with the house; he aimed to see they lived out
their span. When the first tent-moths arrived
and spread their stickiness through the trees,
he began to sweat, to cry out in his sleep.

Those who talked in their sleep, who could not rest,
came to the store each day to visit the druggist,
waited in line for a chance to say what was wrong.
Wednesday afternoons he closed, like the bank,
and stayed in the back room, counting the stock.
He knew she would be lounging on the bedclothes,
talking to some drummer who stands by the door,
who wants a cigarette now but lacks the nerve
to light one up. She would tell about her husband,
how he killed moths and butterflies in a jar;
the man would begin pulling on his pants.
The druggist tilts a line of pills into a box,
tells the boys to be sure and sweep the ceiling,
he is going home now, there are chores to do.

Going home after practice, doing the chores—
those things kept me busy. When the war started
the state widened the road to four lanes,
chopped down the trees in front of his house.
But even before that, when he first retired,
and she was long dead, of some illness,
and I, his grand-nephew, was left there
on summer mornings, for him to look after—
even then I guessed at what had happened:
when he would gather up the old tools
and get a worn-out broom down from the loft
and go out to burn the caterpillar nests
where they clotted the trees. When I watched him
make harsh changes in the way things were.

21

Change made him harsh. Things got in the way
of what he saw and heard. It took a long time
for him to tie the rags about the broom,
soak them in coal oil, then strike a match
and hoist the fuming torch into the air,
touching it here and there among the leaves
where moths were dreaming. I saw them burst
and fall in a bright rain against the grass.
And when the trees were purged, and he stood
with hair and eyebrows full of soot, calling,
pointing toward the branches above, saying how
they were safe now, the fire had healed them,
and when I grew up, I could do it too—
I knew she was not dead, she had run away.

I learned one does not run away from death:
it comes like a harsh glare billowing darkness.
When I went back, after the war, and stopped
at the café next to the bank, no one there
remembered me, though they recalled his name.
"He drove his car onto the tracks one night,"
a farmer said. "Those Nickel Plate tracks
are gone now, all the way to Windfall.
You can hunt rabbit on the old right-of-way
and not worry about some train hitting you.
That whole stretch has come up in wild cherry;
last year the trees were thick with moths."
"I remember him now," the feedstore man said.
"He was a druggist. Had a storefront building."

Rushlights

Homemade candles each consisting of the pith of a rush
dipped in tallow.

To the memory of my father.

They might have known such things, but all too often
they listened for a while, and then forgot—the sound
of water pouring through the mill-race; a clock wound
with a brass key; a last nail hammered in the coffin.

Of your own footfall, nothing stays, yet in the years
since you've been gone, I've sought out ways to follow
moments we both shared, that left no trace. A swallow
banks high above the vanished barn; an owl draws near.

On summer evenings I have gone out riding, roaming
along the western road—have drifted through the husk
of lost towns, where the stagecoach still stops at dusk,
where a stump lantern lights the way in the gloaming.

And once, when I came to the crossroads at Milton,
where four houses stood, one on each corner, I heard
a fiddle's scraping, and the caller clapping hard,
and knew a wake or a wedding was about to begin—

and rode past tiers of windows filled with rushlights
marking some high moment there, some memorable sadness
or joy that only live music and dancing could bless—
that, and the burning of candles long into the night.

Not far beyond the town, in the dark, the horse and I
were lost, carrying that brightness within us, until
it faded at last, and we reached the top of a hill.
I looked out and saw our way through the night sky.

The Purpose of Poetry

This old man grazed thirty head of cattle
in a valley just north of the covered bridge
on the Mississinewa, where the reservoir
stands today. Had a black border collie
and a half-breed sheep dog with one eye.
The dogs took the cows to pasture each morning
and brought them home again at night
and herded them into the barn. The old man
would slip a wooden bar across both doors.
One dog slept on the front porch, one on the back.

He was waiting there one evening
listening to the animals coming home
when a man from the courthouse stopped
to tell him how the new reservoir
was going to flood all his property.
They both knew he was too far up in years
to farm anywhere else. He had a daughter
who lived in Florida, in a trailer park.
He should sell now and go stay with her.
The man helped bar the doors before he left.

He had only known dirt under his fingernails
and trips to town on Saturday mornings
since he was a boy. Always he had been around
cattle, and trees, and land near the river.
Evenings by the barn he could hear the dogs
talking to each other as they brought in
the herd; and the cows answering them.
It was the clearest thing he knew. That night
he shot both dogs and then himself.
The purpose of poetry is to tell us about life.

Two

Mississinewa Reservoir at Winter Pool

A reservoir's not like a lake;
it depends on how much water's
coming in. When it goes down,
in the fall, you can see where

the town used to be—brick
foundations, chunks of concrete,
things still not worn away.
Sunday afternoons in October

the people who lived there once
come back, drive their cars
down to where the road breaks off.
They walk out toward the river.

Nothing remains. The walls of the houses
are gone, the school, the church.
There are no flowers, no trees;
even the cemetery has been moved.

And yet they have come home again,
nothing can harm them now.
They walk to and fro, stopping
to speak, nodding, as though

having risen from a deep sleep
and come at last to a place
no longer having anything in it
except themselves. And as though always.

Poem Written on a Line from the *Walam Olum*

> There at the edge of all the water where the land ends . . .

I was not certain she would meet me there.
Go first and wait, she said, down at the edge
below the bend, where the road forks, and all
the cattails are brown and blown, and water
backed up in the creek makes a dark land
where no one ever goes. You'll see both ends

of a caved-in barn on the left. The property ends
at the barbed wire, but go on from there—
look for a path through the marsh, to higher land
where you come out in cottonwoods, and the edge
of the bluff where you stand shows dark water
moving so slowly it seems not to move at all.

This mound was where the village stood, and all
you see from here, she said, to the far ends
of the clearing, they built up from the water
passing below us now. The mussels down there
were edible then, and at the river's edge
they cracked the shells and tossed them on the land.

She had come up to stand beside me. Island,
really, she said, when the rains come, and all
the lowlands flood. No way to get an edge
on anything here. When the grant money ends
I'll go back to the college. Nothing there,
I'll tell them, nothing near that dark water

worth digging for. They've flown over water
from here to the Ohio, they think the land
can't hide a single site from them. There
should be places people can't find at all.
She folded up her shirt, unhooked the ends
that held her bra, and stepped back through the edge

of shade beneath the trees. A thinner edge
of sunlight showed her body like whitewater
gleaming. Nothing done well ever ends,
she said, touching my hand, not even land
built up one act at a time, so that all
that went before, and after, still waits there.

Then there was movement, as though the land
were water, without edge or ends, and all
I hoped to find or know was gathering there.

Panorama

Even while my grandfather was still alive we used
odd pieces to patch the chicken house—it was better
than store-bought roofing, he always said. Sometimes
he would send me out to the log cabin, with a knife
in the shape of a hawk's bill, to cut off a strip
he happened to need to fix a leak on the barn
or one of the smaller buildings. Tracing the air
with his forefinger, he would draw the outline
of the square or rectangle he wanted. As I walked
through the gates and down the lane I would make
the same figure in the space ahead of me, as a way
of remembering.
                Sometimes at night when they argued,
he threatened to burn the whole thing, just to save
on wood, but she would begin to scold him as a man
of no culture, someone who could not keep a promise:
though it had been her own father who found the body
in the drift, the third morning after the blizzard
of eighty-eight. The horses were gone. The sheriff
and the undertaker came the next day. The dead man
turned out to be a teamster from Indianapolis,
but the ticket wired to the load had blown away.
Her father was allowed to take the wagon back
to his barn, where later the Methodist minister
pronounced the long rolls to be a traveling show,
an exhibition that, when spread out and set up
in a large hall, would create some vast illusion
such as the battlefield at Gettysburg, or Waterloo,
or worse.
           The viewer stood within a huge drum
of artifice and paint designed to fool the eye
and tempt the soul. Better to burn it instantly—
except that its owners might pay to get it back.
Inquiries were made, but notices in the papers
in Dayton and Chicago brought no reply. No one

showed up to claim the two dozen rolls stacked
lengthwise in the bedroom of the original cabin.
Her father, being a devout man, allowed no one
to unroll them; being honest, he considered it
his duty to keep them until they were called for.

But as winters were harsh, and the snows deep,
now and then he would slice off a strip to stuff
in some drafty place, or behind a loose clapboard.
His daughter never realized how her own children
carved off chunks to go sledding with in winter,
or to chink the rough log rafts they launched
each summer on the creek. Fragments of canvas
found their way into town, to fill cracks, to keep
ice-cream cool. Except in the family, no one cared
what the spectacle had been. The smallest square
gleamed with color, thick with the slash of some
impetuous brush.
                    Years ago an old uncle told me
how late one summer evening he and several cousins
got drunk, and carried out the last uncut roll
and spread it on the grass, by moonlight, to see
what they could make of its secrets. "Horses,"
he explained, "with shiny hooves, and banners
flying, and flashes of bright metal, all mixed
together in a kind of drifting smoke or fire.
It was too dark to grasp it all. If the moon
had been full, or a shooting star had lit up
the sky, we still might not have understood
exactly what it was—though whether because
the view itself was incomplete, and needed
to be seen upright, or whether we were simply
drunk and ignorant, and having too much fun,
I couldn't say."
                    There was another story, too,
among women in the family, that certain aunts
had made their own inspection of a long roll,
and would not speak of what they saw. "Eden"

was a word sometimes called out in sleep by one
of these sisters, though no one in the township
answered to that name. Others thought the word
might have been "evening," or possibly "evil."
A few more years, and there was no one left
to talk about such tales.
                                        After his mother's death,
my father wrote, saying that he had gone out
to get the cabin ready to sell, having decided
to burn the last few scraps of canvas, whatever
remained, but found instead the empty bedroom
with its puncheon floor, and the hulls of nuts
scattered by squirrels, and the huge rolls gone
entirely.
                   Years later, while sorting through
his desk, to settle his affairs, I turned up
a six-inch strip of canvas, its edges jagged
and brittle, bits of blue paint flaking away,
the surface indecipherably whorled. I held it
in my hand.
                      For a moment I was up on the barn
with my grandfather, and he laid down his hammer
and began to draw a figure in the air, this time
forming a window with his tracing. I looked through
and saw the farm as it had always been—the lane
I walked along, the metal gates, the woods beyond;
and all around us, where we knelt—and on the roofs
of corn crib and chicken house, tractor shed
and main house, too, with its curved verandah,
where random strips of yellow, orange, and silver
had been nailed—were colors that showed against
the gray of shingles, yet had been transformed
by sun and wind and rain, each ragged piece become
part of a larger pattern—recognizable now,
and lasting, but no more attainable than before.

The Sprinkle House at Busro Creek

In 1809 the Shakers established a settlement called
West Union, at Busro Creek on the Wabash River,
in Indiana Territory. There they brought under
cultivation a two-thousand-acre tract subsequently
known as Shaker Prairie. During the next few years
they set up a distillery, a gristmill, and a sawmill.

By 1820 they had constructed a three-story brick
community house having twenty-five rooms, twenty-
one fireplaces, and two kitchens (one for the women
and one for the men). The following year they built
a meeting house across the road from the dwelling
house.

An epidemic of malaria forced the Shakers to give up
the settlement in 1827. The meeting house alone was
left standing. For many years it was thought to be a
frame structure, but when it was torn down in 1875,
workmen discovered brick walls between the studs.

The present Sprinkle House was built with these
salvaged brick. A square, two-story residence in the
Federal style, it now stands abandoned and open to the
weather on a gravel road five miles west of Oaktown,
a small farming community north of Vincennes.

Though we are gone for eight-score years, this place—
this ruined hearth, bricks slipping from the walls—
is struck from what we saw: as though each face

that witnessed here were laid in tiers, all
joined as one. However strange that seems
to you who stand here now, hearing the call

of mourning dove and the slow, steady stream
and hum of workers bringing the honeyflow
to the beech tree, only remove the beam

from your own eye, soften your heart, and know
we are your neighbors still. Would this be
lasting, this clover, this wind that blows

through the broken windowframes, if we
found refuge solely in each other? We gave
our all to God, and to Mother Ann Lee;

for them we danced, and not ourselves. To save
was never our intent, but to become
true children of an earthly Zion. No grave

could hold that dream. Now that you've come
this far, rest in the shade and stillness,
walk here alone, notice the print of thumb

and finger on the scove-fired brick, guess
what songs we sang going out to the fields
each workday morning. Let your footsteps press

and sink in the mole-haunted grass, feel
earth's give and take. This is the race
we entered, and for your sake, won: the real.

Foundling

for Selene

I would be safe there; she would look after me now.
When the cart drove off, she showed me sweet alyssum
growing among the flagstones, and called it with names
learned from her own grandmother—madwort, heal-bite,
gold-dust, basket-of-gold. In the house, in the room
with the oak cupboard, I would have my own bed. Later,
when company came, and they thought I had fallen asleep,
I heard them speak of a love child in the neighborhood,
whose parents had gone away. I wanted to comfort it—
longed to call out to them that I would be its mother.

Next morning she made cinnamon toast and cambric tea.
They had invited me to visit them all. I ran across
to the house of the two doctors—father and daughter,
homeopathic practitioners—who promised to fetch me
on their trips through the woods, who said I could carry
their long-handled baskets, and help pick hibiscus
and lemon grass, and seek out charms for bee sting
and balm for sunburn—but they were gone already,
in the morning cool, searching along the riverbank.
No one remained who could tell me how love had children.

Next, to the widow's house, by the water's edge,
to wait on the screened-in porch for their return,
finding a place to sit among stacks of magazines,
watching her trim strawflowers to bind for drying,
saying aloud the words she taught me—immortelle
and everlasting—and going out to her garden full
of unfading things: helping her gather up armloads
of ruby and amber cockscomb, stripping the leaves
from the stalks, bringing them back to the porch
to hang in great rippled bunches, dusky and velvet.

I heard them singing harmony, coming along the path.
When I asked, neither of them knew where the love child
had gone, but both affirmed I had not been dreaming.
We are children of nature, they said, therefore of love;
we rise up perennial, like tansy, or hearts-ease, or phlox,
some meant for healing, others for beauty. Our lasting
is seasonal, takes time, becomes life itself, is love.
All that autumn, they said, I could watch the cockscomb
giving itself away in seeds that fell to the newspaper.
Each day I could write my name in its last, best gift.

Over the years I grew and prospered in that green place
always shining with light from the river, that world
that is gone now, under the waters, and cannot return.
During the day I was joined with their stories; and once,
during feigned sleep, I heard those same voices whisper
the names of my real mother and father, who loved each other,
who left their mark on my own flesh as one might draw
words in the sandbank of a stream, or a fresh snowfall.
Over the years I remember the willows shading those walkways,
the gardens we tended, the flowers we gave to each other.

Isinglass

for Glen Buzzard

That was the last word I heard you say
in the white room, at the nursing home,
        when I leaned over your bed
to see if you could recognize me
                and saw instead
that we were standing out on the ice
above Monument City, in January, with
enough gear to last us till nightfall
                and I watched you
brush back the snow, and take an axe
and begin to chop
                until you reached water
and we could look down and see
the streets of the old town spread below us
                like the afterimage
of an isinglass flower gleaming in the door
of an iron stove, when you look away
        and rest your eyes
                on the cool of a white wall.

        All those mornings
that first summer after the dam was built,
when we used to anchor a hundred yards west
of the island
        we could see all the way
to the bottom, to bits and pieces of windowpane
                and mirror
        and other things still shining there—
all that time
        I never thought of diving;
                we were close enough.

And last winter, visiting that place alone,
in March, with the water down as far as it goes

and the piers of the old bridge showing,
I looked out and thought I saw you
                    in a mackinaw coat
and hip boots, a shovel in your hand,
out walking across the mud flats
        where there is nothing
                    nothing at all—

saw you hunched beneath the earphones
of a metal detector,
                    listening, heading
into a cold wind
        waving the wand back and forth
                    above that emptiness,
beckoning to the earth,
                    calling its name
        hearing it answer,
                    knowing
everything returns
            going forward to greet it.

Cicadas

Only one, and then many, scissoring
through the summer dusk, neither calling
nor answering but simply singing—
all risen from the earth, from years
of darkness inexplicable, from dust—
all having labored toward the sun
and left their nether selves behind,
their dry shells clinging—all gone
at last among the leaves, to make music
into the evening, vibration that comes
from within, that emerges, that unfolds
with wavering crescendo, and nothing—
no one, not the great cellist in the hall,
not the sound of the freight train
bearing down on you at the crossing,
no, not even the sigh of the beloved,
safe in your arms a final time,
beginning to call your name—can rise
like this, or fall away so swiftly.

Three

Barn Siding

It can fetch a dollar a board foot
with the right customer, but I've seen
all the old barns I'm going to mess with
for a while. Got no more need for them.

There's no reason for a man my age
taking risks. Time to pay attention
to what's happened in your life, maybe
pass it along to someone younger.

I never got past eighth grade. Never
worked inside, or had to wear a tie,
or sat at a desk. Learned what I know
the hard way. It helps you remember.

When you get in trouble is when you
start to forget. It happened to me,
looking for barnwood. I got greedy,
forgot what I had learned years before:

if you're putting up kiln-dried lumber
and something starts to crack or splinter,
you've got time to get out of the way;
but old wood won't give any warning.

You take a barn or farmhouse that's stood
a hundred years or more, it's had time
to gravitate, work out all the stress.
The wood's cured; got no more surprises.

Tamper with that balance, and you've got
problems. A house will talk to itself
when the sun hits it, or a cold wind;
it tries to adjust. You've got to hear.

That's what you need in this business: ears.
A picker's always going in places
where he shouldn't be. Has to listen,
know when something's about to happen.

What does a picker do? Picks over
what other people have left behind.
Attics. Basements. Sheds. Like this old place
I knew about in Prophet Township.

There was a woods around it. The bridge
a mile up the road had been out
for years. Nobody came along there
anymore. I kept an eye on it

for a long time. I let others have
first choice. Couples from town like to park
along country lanes. Boys with rifles
come shoot out all the windows. Hoboes,

people who start fires. Old house burns
in a place that far out, no one comes.
Maybe you look across the fields some night,
see a red glow way off in the sky.

I heard the barn didn't burn. Gave it
a few more years, let the new trees get
a toe hold. Let the grapevines grow thick.
Then one day I drove out there to see.

What you're looking for is siding with
no color, it's just gone natural
from all that weather. Sometimes the nails
have rusted clear through. You can pry off

big long, smooth pieces with your bare hands.
It's dry, and limber, like old leather
that's been cured right. Every board has what
interior decorators call

"character." If you had gotten up
before daylight and gone out to milk
half a dozen cows, day in, day out
for thirty-odd years, you might call it

something else. But it doesn't matter.
Most of that wood turns out to be pine,
it's full of knots and scattered nail holes,
places where rust has darkened the grain.

I'd been out there all day by myself,
tromping a path through the grass and weeds,
had half a load of tongue-and-groove boards
stacked in the pick-up. Stopped now and then

to try the blackberries growing wild
right up to the double doors. No one
living on that place for thirty years,
limestone chimney where the house had been.

I kept on working. Late afternoon
I took a pair of gloves and a pry-bar
and climbed all the way up to the loft.
Half the floorboards weren't even nailed down.

I fixed up a place to slide them out
a window, took it slow, dropped one plank
at a time down onto the horseweeds.
I'd been up there maybe half an hour,

thought I saw something move. Didn't hear
a thing, just noticed this shadow drift
across the north wall. Sometimes you freeze
before you've had time to think: maybe

it's a mud-dauber hanging there near
your face. Other times your body knows,
takes over, goes where it wants to go,
always brings you out the quickest way.

Even so, I've wondered why that barn
made no noise at all: queen posts starting
to fold in on themselves, rafters, joists,
all those cedar shakes, tons of dry wood

held together for a hundred years,
all beginning to boil, like a storm
brewing, but no thunder, no more sound
than wind making circles in the grass.

I like to think there was nothing left
that could speak, except the wood itself,
everything else was already gone—
grain bin empty, all the old harness

stolen, someone had even climbed up
on the roof to get the lightning rods.
That kind of rod held a big glass ball
people used to say would turn sky blue

from all the current running through it.
You've walked through old houses, or places
that have burnt: nothing but broken cups,
bits of glass, corncobs, heaps of ashes.

Makes you wonder why people would up
and leave a place like that. What happened,
why nobody can make the land pay,
why it all comes up in second growth.

All you hear are stories. This family
tried and lost, that man wore himself out,
this man went out to the barn during
the sale, put a shotgun in his mouth.

You never know why. And there's never
anyone left to tell by the time
some picker stops by to have a look;
there's usually nothing left at all.

There was nothing on this place except
the barn, and nothing left in the barn
except the wood. It had been there all
that time, waiting for the right moment.

Something was holding it together,
some old balance, but when I got down
and pried up that last board, and pushed it
over the edge, the balance was gone

and the whole building simply started
turning itself inside out. It was
a spiked barn, and here and there rain had
gotten in, and turned those handmade nails

to rust. They lost their grip. Everything
started to slip, unravel, come loose
while I was standing there, and I might
be there still, if it hadn't been for

some part of me that was already
heading toward the ladder and the flight
of stairs down to the ground. Everything
got brighter as I ran, all the cracks

between the siding started to glow
and swell with light. Not a trace of wind,
no tornado screaming through the trees,
sucking on the walls, only layers

of dust and chaff that had built up all
those years working free now and spilling
through the light, leaking, spreading like smoke,
making no more sound than a whisper.

I came down the stairs through dust so thick
I couldn't see. I had almost reached
the barn door when a stray board caught me
across the neck—same place I broke it

twenty years ago, up at the lake—
and drove me straight on through the briars.
That was all that saved me: whatever
breaks is always stronger where it mends.

I don't know how long I was out. When
I came to, it was near dark, and still.
I couldn't move. Paralyzed. The barn
was down. There was nothing I could do,

nobody else knew I was out there.
It might be days, maybe even weeks,
before anybody came that far
and noticed the truck parked in the weeds.

I listened and tried to think. No birds,
that's all I could remember. Pigeons,
sparrows, nothing like that in the loft
when I first went up there. Animals

have a way of knowing. They say cows
will lie down before an earthquake hits.
I listened now. There was a cricket
somewhere in the middle of the barn,

or what used to be the barn, and now
was only a mass of lumber and scrap
no higher than a man. A cricket
first, and then a katydid, somewhere

out in the middle of all that wood.
There were lightning bugs, too, I saw them
winking on and off all around me,
but I couldn't move from where I fell.

I thought I would die then, and be like
everything else, even like the barn,
sinking back into the earth. I felt
peaceful; I could hear all the peepers

and tree frogs and night creatures singing
the way they do every summer night.
They made a sound I had always known
and not thought much about. Now I heard.

They were going to take the barn back,
everything that lived out in that woods—
'possums and squirrels and snakes and bugs.
Now that I thought about it, they were

pickers too, just like me. They came out
when no one else was around, and picked
through whatever happened to be there.
They'd take me too. It wouldn't be long.

When it got dark I could look up through
the blackberry canes and maple leaves
at the stars. They say a man's whole life
runs before him when it's time to die.

I remembered my mother coming
to get me out of bed once, waking
me up so we could go out and see
the northern lights. It was a rare sight

that far south. She held me up, pointing
into the sky. I heard her talking
to my father. They were still young then,
there was something in their voices. What

the northern lights looked like I couldn't
remember. All I could see were stars.
I liked her holding me, and him near.
I looked up at the stars now, lying

on my back, without moving, staring
straight up. They were all still there. The more
I looked the more I could see it's not
really up, at all, but out. We look

out and into. We see from a place
that floats through all that, like a lantern
carried in the dark. I knew no one
would come and find me, but I thought how

you lift the globe, and put in a match,
and the light gives off smoke, until you
turn down the wick, and adjust the flame.
Lower the globe; and now you're all set

to go out and find whatever's lost.
Starting to fall asleep in the dark
I thought I saw something glimmering
like a wick catching fire, like the light

in the barn when it started to shake.
It was daylight, morning. My father
and I were climbing up the steep roof
on our own barn to free a kite stuck

on the weathervane. We threw it down
and then went on to the end. I saw
the lightning rod up close, got to touch
the iron, all scarred and encrusted,

then bent over to look through the ball
of glass the grounding cable ran through.
For a moment I saw everything
through the blue of that ball—down below

the pasture, the creek winding through it,
the four milk cows wading in the smoke
of the willows, the sky reflecting
on the water, the water and grass

and clouds all blue, the whole world blue
as though it had always been that way
and I had never known till I got
to see it through the lightning rod's eye.

I saw it again, lying there, not
able to move—that same blue world,
full of stars now. It was the last thing
I saw before sinking into sleep.

When I woke the next day, I was still
a child, this time looking up at
my own face in a mirror: it moved,
smiled, gazed back at me. Disappeared,

so I could see trees and sky again.
Saw part of her shoulder, then her face
moving around above me, circling,
doing a little dance, looking down

but saying nothing. I tried to speak
but my lips were frozen, no words came.
Help, help, I said in my mind, go get
help, but she was farther away now

and then everything was still. Child.
Little girl. What was she doing here?
Was there anyone with her? and soon
I heard the old woman's voice coming

closer: she was picking her way through
the canes, grumbling when they stuck to her,
sometimes setting the tin buckets down
to get free, warning the child against

spilling berries they'd already picked.
Then it was her face, looking in mine
to see if I was dead or alive,
and seeing something worse than a ghost,

something that had mattered even more
to her than living or dying, once,
a long time ago—me, my own face
but thirty years later now, grown old,

gone sunken and pale, like a wax face
in a coffin. I could see her eyes
while she looked down at me, studying
what to do, even what to say now.

I'd not seen her since that first evening
I got back in fifty-six, after
two years in Korea. Her folks had
lived out on this place; her dad farmed it.

She and I rode the same schoolbus;
on rainy days we played in the barn.
And when I joined the Army, she said
she would wait for me, she wrote letters

all that time, and said she was saving
herself for me, that we could get married,
but my younger brother wrote and said
she was going out with other guys.

My first night home we went out to park
in my brother's car. I took off all
her clothes and said now since you've saved it
for me I want it the way the whores

do it in Japan and she started
to cry while I took her on her knees
and made her cry even more and then
pushed her out the door and drove off

with all her clothes. I never knew how
she got home, never saw her again
after I got my discharge papers.
I heard they moved to another state.

And now here she was, it was her, make
no mistake, even with all the lines
and creases and crow's-feet—I could tell.
I could hear her breath coming hard while

she looked down at me, trying to think
what to do next, not even certain
I was still alive. I couldn't blink
or move my eyes. I think she touched me,

touched my face, my body, then my wrist,
feeling for a pulse. I'm still alive,
I tried to say, get me out of here,
I didn't mean it, I'm sorry, I'll

make it up to you somehow, after
all these years. Now she was looking straight
at me. She reached out to touch my face.
"Tears," she said, speaking for the first time.

"Tears. You bastard. Thirty years later
and you're crying." She moved back, out of
my range of vision. I heard her talk
to the little girl, who must have been

a mute. She stood over me again.
Evidently I was still crying—
tears of happiness that she would go,
come back with help, bring an ambulance,

medics, rescue team. "We're going now,"
she said simply. "It won't do to keep
fresh blackberries out in warm weather."
They moved off through the weeds, carrying

both buckets, going slow, bending back
the canes. Everything got calm again.
It was still early morning. I knew
for certain I was going to die now,

and it seemed all right this time, not much
I could do about it anyway.
I started drifting, having dreams with
nothing in them. Whether I woke up

staring into the sky, or whether
I slept till nightfall, I never knew.
Sometime in the night I entered shock;
I was unconscious the next morning.

I had no life signs when they found me
that afternoon, after I had been
lying there for almost two whole days.
Medics came in a helicopter

to lift me out of there, take me down
to a hospital in the city.
They told me all this later, after
I spent a week in intensive care.

There's always a moment, when you first
wake up in a bright room, with nurses
wearing white dresses and little hats,
you think you've died and gone to heaven;

I wasn't dead yet, but I came close.
The man who found me came to see me
in my hospital room. He worked for
the State Police, an interpreter

of aerial photographs. They had
been studying satellite photos
of that part of the world, trying
to see where the Interstate Strangler

might have buried more of his victims.
He picked up young hitch-hikers, maybe
offered them money for kinky sex,
took them to abandoned farms not far

off the Interstate. They were handcuffed,
then strangled and mutilated, left
in shallow graves and covered with brush.
They had found seven graves at four sites

and they were looking for more. Sometimes
a fresh grave shows up on a photo
taken by a satellite. Sometimes
they spot a suspicious vehicle

in an unlikely place, or make out
tracks worth investigating. This man
had an old photo that showed the barn,
and a brand-new one that showed the barn

changed, in some way, and my pick-up parked
at the end of an untraveled lane,
on a farm they already knew was
abandoned, on their list to watch close.

They sent a team out right away with
guns drawn in case it was the Strangler
holed up there, and of course they found me
in his place. My paralysis was

only temporary. I walked out
of that hospital a week later,
a bit stiff but still able to climb
in my truck—the troopers brought it there—

and drive home. They had confiscated
the half load of barn siding but dropped
the trespassing charge. The county paid
the Medivac for rescuing me,

the state picked up the tab for my stay
in the hospital. I don't know why—
maybe they added it to the cost
of catching the Strangler. They got him

a month later—by that time they knew
he drove a pick-up, and this was in
all the newspapers and on TV.
A driver on the Interstate saw

a hitch-hiker get in a pick-up
and memorized the license number
and phoned it in to the State Police
from the next rest-stop. The Strangler

gave up after a high-speed chase through
three counties. They say he'll get the chair.
Me, I gave up picking barn siding.
I work strictly on old houses now,

sometimes garages. There's a demand
for copper; the price is going up.
I can rip it out of those old walls,
those basements, better than anyone.

I have to listen, pay attention,
like always. I don't want those shadows
sneaking up on me again. Sometimes
I think I died out there in the weeds

next to where that barn fell in, and I'm
a different person now, born again
but in a strange way. Sometimes I think
it was God who looked down through the lens

of that satellite camera and
saw me lying there. Sometimes I think
it was me who looked out through the eye
of the lightning rod, and saw something

that might have been God. And then there was
Rhetta showing up like that, as though
no time had passed, and how I asked her
to forgive me, even though I knew

she couldn't hear me. For a while
I thought she had left me there to die.
Then I understood it could have been
a lot worse. She might have had a knife

or a pair of pruning shears. No one
would have known. When they found my body,
the coroner would have chalked it up
to the Strangler. She didn't do that,

she simply went away with the girl
and the berries. It's odd to think how
even the Strangler could have passed through
a place like that, looking for something

and not finding it, then moving on.
Nobody's lived on that old farm since
the middle nineteen-fifties, nothing's
left there now but a bunch of trees set

back from the road. The other pickers
will have cleaned up the barnwood by now,
carried it off like a swarm of ants
at a picnic. One of these years when

the freeze-and-thaw works enough mortar
from between the stones, and the chimney
blows over, there won't be anything
left there except the blackberry patch.

People will still stop by—different
kinds of pickers, the ones who know where
the hickory nuts grow, out in the woods,
and where to find the best shaggymanes

and puffballs, and when it's time to look
for morels. Those people are shadows
moving along the edges, always
keeping a step ahead. Finding things

can be a calling, a way of life.
All a picker wants to do is find
something nobody else knows about,
have it for a while, then pass it on.

This story I've been telling you now,
you might say you just ran across it
by accident, but the plain truth is
we don't hear things until we're ready

and that could be a kind of finding,
too, even a way of life—paying
attention to what's happening now,
then handing it on to someone else.

You take those young men the Strangler found
standing at the side of the highway,
or waiting in one of those rest-stops,
hoping for a ride to the next town:

they're no different from the rest of us,
they've come to see there's no going back,
everything is gone now, or changed from
the way it used to be. There's no shame

in what they did. They say he would talk
about helping them out, would tell them
that just past this next exit he knew
of a man who needed a good hand

to work for him for a day or two,
in this old farmhouse, fixing it up,
getting it ready to sell again.
If you hadn't eaten anything

for two or three days, or hadn't slept,
if you were flat broke and couldn't seem
to get a ride, you'd listen to him,
you'd want him to like you, be willing

to go with him while he keeps turning
down those deserted roads, those old lanes
where the signs are full of bullet holes,
where the apple trees have all gone wild.

Then think of the satellite out there
in space mapping that part of the world,
looking down and seeing everything,
catching it just before it changes

but not knowing what anything is—
maybe seeing Rhetta and the child
walking along with their tin buckets,
maybe seeing me sliding old boards

down out of that barn loft, the Strangler
parked in the truck, talking to the boy—
while this shadow drifts out over us,
the one we can never really know.

Four

Interview

Now this here rag is the one they used to call
the lost rag.

Sort of thing everybody knew and nobody ever bothered
to write down.

It was just a few licks, something you'd sit and play
by yourself,

when there was nobody else around. Maybe it was
some old man

showed you how to play it, a long time ago. You turn off
that machine,

I'm going to play it for you now. I said
turn it off.

Drawing the Antique

The Victoria and Albert . . . still displays its great
collection of casts. American art museums destroyed
theirs—the Chicago Art Institute did so, I believe, in
the 1950s—or, as in the case of the Metropolitan
Museum of Art, has them in storage in a highway
viaduct. . . .

Henry Hope Reed, letter to the *New York*
Review of Books, 17 August 1989.

On the third floor of the old high school—
up a stairway fenced off in the late sixties
due to rising costs and squabbles over turf—
through an iron gate, with the principal's key,
down a barrel-vaulted hallway, along doors
nailed shut now, past rows of display cases
displaying nothing—
                        after turning a corner
in our explorations, we come face to face
with three life-sized plaster casts acquired
when the local art league put them up for grabs
back during the fifties.
                        Copies of copies,
on pedestals, their dim, dust-mantled features
glossy in places, luminous in the bleak light:
a Venus of some forgotten school, nipples
rubbed smooth, pudenda hammered and dented;
a wounded gladiator, fallen, overwhelmed
by marking-pencil swastikas; a statesman,
uplifted hand corroded, structural wires
bleeding through.
                        They wait here, faces battered,
noses chipped away, lips stained yellow where
countless cigarette butts, moistened with spit,
were carefully stuck.
                        Left in this dark place,
they become more like their lost originals,

true to some idea we can barely imagine now.
Yet we are shocked, we know them instantly—
recognizable as victims everywhere, shapes
destroyed and timeless,
                          still able to instruct.

This Is Not a Poem

1.

A few American prisoners who survived Hiroshima managed to escape
with the help of Lieutenant Nobuichi Fukui, a devout Christian:

"Gesturing toward the funeral pyres still burning in the city,
he turned to the American soldiers. 'Look there,' he ordered them,
'That blue light is women burning. It is babies burning.
                    Is it wonderful to see the babies burning?' "

2.

"Such stories are by now a part of the oral tradition of Hiroshima,
and they are told and retold as part of the rites of remembrance
            for the 200,000 victims finally claimed by the bomb.

"There are those who speak of an American woman who died in the
            bombing,
or of black soldiers who were held in prison, and died there, too.
Some witnesses report that P.O.W.'s crawled from the rubble,
that one of them was stabbed and that others
                    were taken to a drill field, there to be shot.

"Most often of all, witnesses recount the story of a young American man,
the third confirmed survivor of the blast (with Neal and Brissette),
who was beaten to death on the morning after the bomb was dropped.
Witnesses describe him as 'the handsomest boy I ever saw,'
            with 'blond hair,' 'green eyes,' 'white waxlike skin,'
                    'a big body, and very strong, looking like a lion.'

"They say that he was tied to a pole with a note that read
            'Beat This American Soldier Before You Pass,'
and that he was then stoned and clubbed to death
by a crowd on Aioi Bridge, where the Enola Gay had set its sights."

3.

That is all; this is not a poem. It is simply the last paragraph
of an article in *The New York Times Magazine* for 2 December 1984,

which tells of American prisoners who lived and died in that city.
Conscientious reporters worked for years
                              to find out what happened to them.

There is nothing more. A poem could only enhance, celebrate;
here there is nothing to be admired. Nothing we can do—
tear out these pages, carry them around in our billfolds, make copies,
mail them to other persons we know—none of that matters.

Notice instead that the last young soldier managed to do
what none of us has managed, what each of us still faces
              every day of our lives, every morning, every hour—
he had survived The Bomb. And yet a mob still came for him.

This is not a poem. It is brave reporting; it invites you
to think about the task before us even after The Bomb is dismantled,
after we have taken it apart and beaten it into plowshares.

It asks how we shall live, even then.
                              A poem asks how we shall live now.

Head of the God of the Number Zero

The Blood of Kings, Plate 110
Copan, Honduras
Late Classic period, CE 770–780
Stone, 102.7 x 35.3 cm
The Cleveland Museum of Art

"Rendered in nearly three-dimensional form,
the head of a god emerges from the wall
of a building." On his brow, notice the swarm,
rendered in nearly three-dimensional form,
of rattlesnake rattles. His bound hair warns
he will be sacrificed and yet not fall—
rendered in nearly three-dimensional form,
the head of a god emerges from the wall.

He watches empty space, precisely shown:
the hand beneath his chin is seconds away
from ripping off his jaw. Without a groan
he watches. Empty space, precisely shown
by emblems all about his face, is stone
proclaiming nothingness. Beyond decay,
he watches empty space. Precisely shown,
the hand beneath his chin is seconds away.

Nothing has meaning now except the dream
in the head of the god of the number zero—
that one of us might waken to his scream,
"Nothing has meaning now!" Except the dream
does not end when we turn away. The gleam
in his eye is not that of victim, but hero.
Nothing has meaning now except the dream
in the head of the god of the number zero.

On the Back Doorstep

In this, the last decade of the twentieth century, plants
and animals are now experiencing from 1,000 to 10,000
times the normal rate of extinction.
                  Biodiversity specialist, Harvard University

The right talon broken, two claws extended, two bent back,
          the left still clenched, but holding to nothing now:
each dark hook knotted and bunched, like twisted wire,
          each narrowing to an unretractable sliver of nail.
The slash of charcoal pinfeathers across the throat,
          scatter of dalmatian spots along the barrel chest;
the left wing, when extended, perfectly elastic and yielding,
          the quills bright orange, the vanes dull gold
out toward the tips, then yellow and gray intermingled,
          becoming gradually—at the joint with the body—
a creamy fluff. The wing itself still supple, interlocking,
          so that it is easy to imagine the movement, the sweep
of expansion and contraction, the flickering of shadow
          among the magnolia branches. Turn it over, study
the broad back, the bold stripes—alternating pattern
          of black and gray—on the folded wings; the crest
on top of the head, red as new paint, the bill tapered
          to a flat point, like a nail-set. The eyes gone.

For an Old Flame

When the news came, there was nothing left,
none of those old trappings. When you spoke,
no sound emerged. I knew it was neither dream
nor vision—those categories had broken down,
nothing remained. You stood somewhere
in a junkyard—surrounded by piles
of rusted and broken bodies, doors gone,
engines disemboweled, windows shattered—
where they had brought your compact car
after the head-on collision. Here
you had come too, inevitably, since
the dead have no other place to go
in this world we have made: nothing waits
beyond, no light escapes from the horizon
of physical events. Occasionally
a couple of teen-age boys wander by,
with vise-grips and adjustable wrenches,
looking for cheap parts for their dragster.
Here you could stay forever, unnoticed
among the mountains of rust and old rubber,
the soiled back seats, the glove compartments
with their forgotten artifacts. It remains
only for me to set you now in the prow
of an all-black '57 Chevrolet hard-top
with dual carburetors and a glass-packed
muffler, and pay the ferryman the coins
from your eyes, and see you start out,
not looking back, over those dark waters.

Frieze

1.

What others might call mud, or sludge, at the bottom
of this cave, is a way of keeping time. Here

stone dissolves, drop by drop, and forms again,
half an inch every thousand years. Fish with dead eyes

drift through dark pools. Dust, sediment, pollen,
insects pursued by salamanders, frogs by shrews—

a slow rain, over the edge, into the deepest holes.
Two spelunkers, having lowered themselves into

a room far inside the earth, where nothing else
has ever entered and left, find a fragment of bone

preserved by the seep of minerals changing places,
but worked free now—a moment in sunlight, remembered.

2.

Others join them. They stake off the site, brush back
years, centuries, until the curve of the vertebrae

starts to show, the splay of ribs cracked by the fall.
They call for more gear to be lowered down—

cameras, a line from a generator, banks of lights—
and continue to trace, out of the hardened silt

and debris of the last five millennia, the skeleton
of a prehistoric bear that stumbled over the ledge

and landed eighty feet below. Immured, it lived on
for weeks or months, dragging itself through the muck,

groping for a way to escape, listening to reach out
and catch what it could not see. For this broken creature

the transition was total: whatever it knew in light,
it went on doing in darkness. Its presence lingers.

3.
If you turn the floodlight's beam against the walls
you can make out faint claw marks, unevenly spaced—

at first higher than a man can reach, then lower down, wave
upon wave—as the bear kept searching for something

beyond this blackness, for a hold in the rock,
a way to lift itself up toward the next change.

Five

Portrait Studio

Still here, then, the antique letters in gold,
the sun-bleached faces peering through the glass;
all of them still waiting. The old backdrops
have stayed the same, the hand-painted curtains,
you do not have to look twice to see them
standing before those frozen waterfalls,
those cedar boughs, those far peaks capped with snow.
Instead, you climb the staircase wedged between
the dimestore and the drugstore, you go up
into the hallway, the gray corridor,
you find the right words on the frosted pane.
Step in, and the photographer appears,
drying his hands on his apron, just popped
out of the darkroom, no helper today.
In the studio everything is piled
and dim and dusty; it was his father's
before he took it over. The windows
are boarded up with what used to be called
"car siding"—varnished once, but peeling now.
You spin the wooden stool, and sit down.
While he moves the spotlights and reflectors,
while he fusses with the camera angle,
while he asks about your daughter, your eyes
begin to see shapes beyond the brightness,
and you sense that in the finished portrait
he will show you gazing out of shadows
your father knew, even your grandfather.
There will be a patch of light hovering
in the background, just above your shoulders,
and beyond that, toward the edge, a darkness.
Part of what appears there will be painted,
part will be reflection, and part will be
something into which you have been growing
all this time—as though an old cloak, made up
of many folds and gathers, still being
held out for you, almost fitted you now.

Configuration

Glen Cooper Henshaw, American impressionist,
was born in Windfall, Indiana, in 1880 and died
in Baltimore in 1946.

What I first knew of a life of art
was what he touched last—the summer studio
where I was allowed to wander as a child
through high-ceilinged rooms, up stairways
lined with tapestries unraveling: bronzes
gathering dust, wrought candlesticks, rows
of Chinese vases, the August light shuttered
like strands of Aunt Carolyn's uncombed hair,
the huge easels with their unfinished seascapes,
the closets thick with stacks of pastels
where mice made burrows, and damp seeped.

Beginning there, at the last turn
of the stairs, at the view of the Salute
by moonlight, in its great gold frame—
beginning with the packets of letters,
the yellowed clippings, the photograph
with the calico cat perched on his shoulder—
I followed him from farm, school, bistro,
through the sketchbooks of Market Street
and the Lower East Side, the pushcarts
and railroad flats, the life classes
in the blue cold of the old Academy rooms
in Munich, the boat trains to London,
the first commissions and sittings,
the laughter in the salons, the bare shoulders
of the soprano who stands beside the piano,
the young women with braided, coiled hair
lifting their skirts as they come up the stairs,
the afternoons wandering among the bookstalls,
the café conversations with Matisse—
all this rippling from a single stone

and the force that carried it gone, leaving
only the slow parchment whispering
of old voices in nursing-homes, recollections
of places where they met and talked, séances
around an oak table, a picnic at Fontainebleau,
the crowds in Maxwell Street before the War.
Gradually the surface resumes a smoothness:
second wife buried, paintings knocked down
and scattered, studio burned, each letter
traced, each name marked off, finally
only the quiescence of paperwork—index cards
and conjectures, learned comparisons, polite
notes of inquiry from graduate students,
the curator's handwritten invitation for brandy,
spools of microfilm humming in the machine.

What I first perceived, then, wandering alone
among those vanished rooms; what I last
have come to understand, having followed
that trajectory even as it began to merge
with my own: the face in the photograph, taken
when she left Boston to come to him
on the Rue Monsieur-le-Prince
in the springtime of that fresh year,
that new century. Her long auburn hair
enveloping that nakedness, the purl
of gas jets turned down in the hallway,
the bell curve of the lamp chimney
by the bed, the swirled perfection
of her sleeping: the configuration
of time, of love, of youth, of art
like an elaborate watermark visible
only when held up to the light.

Moiré

Up to the present we have not succeeded in pointing to
any difference in the consequences, whether phantasy
or reality has had the greater share in these events of
childhood.

Freud, *Introductory Lectures*, 1916

One of her uncles, she said, who never left home
or married, whose room was on the third floor
of the old house, at the end of a long stairway.
When she and her sisters were small, sometimes
they were sent to stay with their grandparents
for a few days. The uncle came down for meals,
and treated them kindly, and seemed harmless.
He had gone to the university, years before,
and done quite well, and still had textbooks
in his room about Schrödinger and Max Planck
and Heisenberg's principle of indeterminacy.
At dinner he would talk of billiard balls
colliding, of bodies infinitely in motion,
infinitely at rest. Placing the sugar bowl
in the salt shaker's path, he would explain
the differences between Newton and Einstein,
and why nothing travels faster than light,
and what Oppenheimer said to General Groves.
Once each visit he invited them to his room
to look at his universal analytical engine.
He had assembled it himself, over many years,
using parts from player pianos, bicycle
sprockets, unidentifiable joints and gears
from automobile transmissions, and a handle
from an ice-cream freezer. When he turned
the crank, disks and cogs began to catch
and trip still other mechanisms, setting up
a harsh grinding: banks of wheels glittered
and whirled, then locked tight or dropped
into slots, while others continued to spin

and wobble. Leaning down, he would ask it
questions—would the girls have a nice day
at the zoo tomorrow with their grandfather,
or would it rain? Would Governor Dewey
beat President Truman? Was their grandmother
planning to bake a pie, or a chocolate cake?
They could see nothing in the whirring gears,
the random configurations, but the uncle
bent down close, nodding to each reply.
His smallest act was dictated by its findings—
brushing his teeth, making his bed, working
in the garden, bringing in the mail. He spent
most of each evening in his room, asking it
questions. Everyone in the family accepted
his behavior; no one seemed to think it odd.
The girls thanked him for the demonstration,
then went downstairs to join their grandmother
and listen to the radio before going to bed.
"Jack Benny," the youngest sister recalled,
years later, coming to the end of her tale.
"He was our favorite. But we also liked
Fred Allen, and Fibber McGee and Molly."
She told the story only once, and I paid
little attention; people say strange things
about their relatives. The uncle was alive,
even then, somewhere up on the third floor,
consulting his machine. Gradually I forgot
the year, the name of the town where she said
it happened—was it Springfield, Mass.,
or Zanesville, Ohio? Was she a good friend
or a casual acquaintance, someone I had met
for five minutes at a cocktail party? After
all these years, I cannot recall her name,
there is too much static, the story fades
in and out, like an old-time radio show,
like radiation left over from the Big Bang,
undetectable to all but the most
sophisticated equipment. At times it flares—

erupts, even, in my memory; at others
it dwindles and decays, gradually subsiding
into some gray plasma of forgetfulness—
fragments of books and films and concerts,
shadowy faces, recollected afternoons,
everything blurred and run together now,
dim and barely flickering. What was once
a pale ivory sphere, moving through space,
is now a haze of particles, each pattern
peeling back to reveal another, farther off,
deeper within. What remains to be grasped
counts for little more than a flask of numbers
on a shelf above the talcum and the chalk,
in a hall where old men lean down to peer
across a dark green table, half dreaming,
half remembering how the next combination
will fall. In the years since I heard that story,
machines with memories of their own—brains
which churn and whir and crank out answers—
have eliminated the guesswork, the feeling
ahead in the dark. I would like to believe
that somehow, somewhere—out there
in Lansing, or Biloxi, or Great Falls—
a few tinkerers have managed to survive,
have kept working all this time: holed up
in rooms at the ends of long corridors,
laboring by the light of a single lamp,
patiently going over their assemblages,
checking the tolerances, filing the edges.
These days I travel a great deal, driving
alone, back and forth across the country.
Sometimes in the summer when I pass through
Asheville, or Shaker Heights, or Sacramento,
I find myself gazing at roofs and gables
on the older houses—Queen Anne Style,
they call it, or Stick Style: cupolas,
turrets, porches trimmed with gingerbread.
Usually the windows along the upper floors

are not plate glass. Builders learned ways
to skimp: they would lay down pine floors
rather than oak, install cheaper grades
of glass—wavy panes, which yield distortions,
even now, when I look up at the ceilings,
the light fixtures. Everything seems to bend
and blur as I peer through that swirling,
those aimlessly shifting patterns. If only
I could find him, if only I could recognize
the house, the room, there would be questions
I would ask, answers he might be able to give,
after all this time, comforting answers
to simple questions: how the light will fade,
through the trees, as evening comes on; where
to turn, at the highway, in order to find
a place for the night. Whether to stay there,
helping him twist the crank, hearing him tell
of the many voices, the wheels within wheels;
whether any of this is true, whether the woman
who told me the story is still a girl somewhere,
on another floor, in a room where the sisters
are playing dress-up, with a trunk full of gowns
and hats with dark veils. When I open the door,
they have been expecting me, and do not turn
from the mirror, do not look at me directly
but watch, knowing that I am there, standing
in the shadow of the hallway. Whether it is
my own story I am telling, and forgetting,
whether the machine could explain to me how
they have been waiting all this time, waiting
for me to admire their reflections shimmering
in the nacreous light, my face identical now
among their own, all of us veiled and lost
and revealed at last in the mirror's depths—
whether I could walk on down the stairway,
through the quiet rooms, to the porch, and out
across the lawn, under the trees, at dusk,
having accepted everything that has happened

in this life, and everthing that has not:
ways in which forgetfulness and remembrance,
like patterns on a screen, or a high window
glimpsed fleetingly, or from far away, seem
to change and yet not to change, remaining
infinitely at rest, infinitely in motion.

Eidolon

Unsubstantial image; phantom.

They believed the flow of sulphurous water
possessed a subtle power, and could restore,
whether they yielded to immersion in rooms
deep within the bathhouse—
                              long pools lit
from banks of high windows—soft reflections
pulsing mirror-like across the ceiling,
the white-tiled walls—the depths of the water
veined with slow-moving light—
                                or whether
they came outside, on a summer's day, erased
and smoothed by having drifted in that stillness,
and looked up at the sun high in the trees
on the hill above the bandstand, and stood
in the shade of the pavilion at the spring,
with its pillars, its stone steps:
                                  thin stream
issuing from the lion's mouth, the sound
of water falling, overflowing the basin—
all this healed them, gave them back a sense
that had been missing in their lives, something
they hungered for, but could not find.
                                        Now,
they had only to approach, take the tin cup,
hold it out, then drink—
                          And when by chance
I came that way, after everything was gone—
windows boarded up, summer people fled,
the spa forgotten now for fifty years—
and stopped, on a winter's day, with new snow
over the old—and walked down:
                                it was still
flowing, despite the years, undiminished

even in zero weather, and where it spilled
the basin's edge it had turned to ice—reefs
of ice slowly rising and falling, waves
building and dissolving, reaching farther
into space—
                    pure essence made visible
with cold sunlight shining down through it
so that I had to lean against ice, to grasp
its transiency, its nothingness, its grace
in order to put my lips to that clear stream
still issuing forth.

Cecropia Moth

It was only you, come out of the willows, drying your wings
for the first time in something you had never known before—
not the slow glimmer of silk your ghost had wrapped around you,
not the wind's rustle in the branches, but light: I saw it too,

I stood in the same stillness, just after daybreak, thinning
and cutting back the canes of the rose bush in the side yard,
and I noticed your shadow at first—something pulsing there
among the leaves—then looked again, and saw it was you,

that you were waiting for a moment neither of us could tell,
that would only come as the sun rose higher. So I went on
with my work, my pruning and severing, and you continued
with yours, there in the shade, in the half-light of morning.

After I had made a pile of dead canes, I returned to the place
where you had been resting, and looked through the branches,
and saw you were gone. Sometimes I have noticed the shadow
of a hawk's wings on the grass, but looked around too late—

or turned the wrong way—and seen nothing. Nor am I certain,
even now, what came over us. Yet I know it was there—perhaps
when I put a match to the canes, and watched them give off fire,
sudden and fierce, and black smoke, too, all rising together.

For Starr Atkinson, Who Designed Books

Oldest of words, of sounds: star.
Everything of that name perishes.
The sun will reclaim each planet,
the galaxy collapse, light itself
siphon down into a last darkness.

From you I learned how images balance
in the white space of each page,
how pages unfold like leaves,
how light and dark interpenetrate,
how what we do will not be noticed.

Light from those stars coming deep
from space, reaching our own eyes
in darkness, at the top of a hill;
words on a page keeping the old sounds,
the ones worth saying another time.

Six

Seed Storm

Now I know, watching their slow falling,
that the cottonwoods are not simply speaking
but have begun to sing, in their own way,

and that the feathery notes sifting down
all around us on this late May afternoon
are only a dream of snowfall, of weather

we have come through, all of us, everything
that moves or breathes or waves in the wind.
Ahead of us now the whiteness descending

gathers in drifts in the grass and flows
down the pathways, catching at peonies bent
with heaviness, poppies starting to scatter—

and I understand, as though these gestures
were the language of some ancient chorus,
that I have entered my fiftieth summer

walking beneath these trees, all of them
members of the poplar family, whose leaves
still quiver, even when there is no wind.

Look, the air is so calm now the seed storm
no longer seems to fall, while we ourselves
are what is rising, up into that trembling.

The Enchantment

For Jim White, 1936-1981.

In June, early in the month, after rains
had made the ground soft, and darkened
the grass, and a clear wind all day long
kept lifting the tree limbs, and smoothing
their undersides: that day we talked—
stacks of new books ranged before us
on the wicker table, iced-tea glasses
making rings of moisture—and looked out
into the light that shifted with each change
of wind, and glossy leaves that seemed
still half asleep in their slow turning—
and a bumblebee, driven by the breeze,
sailed in from the rosebush near the steps
and held us there, two native Hoosiers
knowing from earliest childhood what to do:
become as statues waiting to be freed
from some invisible enchanter's spell,
and neither speak nor move. So that
a passerby who saw us sitting there
might well have wondered at the sight
of two grown men, eyes closed, heads bowed—
not knowing that the sudden stillness
flowing through each moment is neither
grace, nor prayer, but simply there.

Galleynipper

Where we might go, in the summers, to a cabin on the big lake
and spend time there in the light, my sister and I, doing
nothing, playing in the sand, slowly turning brown and learning
to see through the glare, my mother with her book, her sunbonnet,

and nights in that room of open rafters, curtains drawn against
a cold wind off the bay: if we were good she would let us have
one candle, in a saucer on the deal table, in the exact center
of our bedroom, that we could not touch, but only watch making

shadows among the iron headboards, the rafters, the curved frame
of the mirror: until we saw our own faces, in a strange slow dusk,
swimming out past a point where we would be taken by the waves
and carried under, into a darkness that beat nightlong outside

our window. Not once did I outlast the candle's glimmering,
to know true blackness, but lay there watching through a blur
of lashes, through my own weariness, hearing my sister begin
her even rowing toward that other shore, waiting to see what

insect or flying creature chance might allow in the room
through a crack in the door or a tear in the screen. Watched
how they preened themselves in the light, how they tilted
toward its center: moth the color of sand, midge or miller hatched

out of dust, and about to return, rendered mad now, taking
leave of their senses, erratically orbiting, coming in closer,
changing the shadows too, casting up their own ghosts, adding
to the slow beating carrying me toward sleep—shapes that would be

only a pool of wax and grit by morning, smudge of wick, drift
of gauzy wing caught like amber. But one of those creatures
alone came as though drawn not by flame but by light itself,
content to float back and forth above the beds, the sleeping

sister, and long ago I heard my mother call it by its old
Hoosier name, this pale, slow-moving, slow-beating, hushed fly
or harmless mosquito that seemed undrawn by fire, and hovered
beneath the rafters, or skimmed the walls, as though searching—

galleynipper, she called it, that comes at the wind's rising,
that asks nothing, that is huge and slow and going nowhere
except back and forth in the shadows, that will not hurt you,
that is too wise to believe in a candle or its dark image

guttering, past midnight, in a patched and scaling mirror:
galleynipper, that had come for me, that would carry me high
above the waves, the sleeping figures adrift, even above
the light, and I would know when we had come to the right place.

Double Jacquard Coverlet

In white cotton and blue wool, dated 1844. Attributed to William
Craig, Sr., born in Kilmarnock, Ayrshire, in 1800. As a young man he
was apprenticed to a hand-loom weaver. During the first half of the
nineteenth century he and thousands of fellow craftsmen in the
British Isles and northern Europe were displaced by the advent of
power-driven looms.

Craig emigrated to the United States in 1820. In the years prior to the
Civil War, he made rugs and coverlets at different sites in Decatur
County, Indiana. He worked on a jacquard loom and taught the craft
to two of his sons. After the war, when machine-made products
became more plentiful in the middle-west, the younger Craigs turned
to making their living by farming. William Craig, Sr., died in 1880.

Weavers, each time I come into your country again, I can tell—
    by the changing light, by the thunderheads piled up
far to the west, darkening the sun. Entering your world once more
    I begin to remember, to look out across the level fields,
to notice a luster in the windows of abandoned farmhouses,
    a glimmering along the slate roofs, the brick chimneys.
Out there, beyond stands of oak and yellow poplar, the late sun
    arrows through, and patches of earth begin to glow
with a brilliance that softens and swells in the breeze.
    Old boundary lines stand out, forgotten pastures re-emerge,
and I begin to grasp how you were driven ahead of the storm,
    how you passed this way once, through these same shadows.

For a long time there has been no rain. Far out on the land
    a boy leads a bay horse over the fresh-turned furrows,
and for a moment the figures are lost in a yellow wind
    swirling around them. Suddenly the horse rears
through the smoke, trying to break away, but across the field
    a bearded man comes running, calling to the beast
in a soothing tongue—and out of the shifting wind all three
    step forth, as though from a cloud, into new light,
the man leading the horse, the boy at his side. In that instant
    they are lifted, borne up by strands come together,
drawn ahead of the storm by an old knowledge, through brightness
    grown steady now, blooming and blossoming at their feet.

"What is that wind that gathers behind us, father, what name
         did you give to the horse? How can he walk to the barn
so calmly, why is this place so filled with light?" Even now
         I would reach out to them, my fingers catch at thistles
waving along the border, but the wind quickens, carrying me away,
         carrying the coverlet too, turning it over completely
until everything is reversed . . . a kettleful of blue flowers,
         simmering for a hundred years, scattering afterimages
across a sky of indigo and rainwater . . . a hand reaching to draw
         the coverlet's heaviness over me, torrents of darkness
battering the slate roof. I flow toward your landscape, weavers,
         your colors rinsed from roots, from the barks of trees.

The way of my coming here no longer matters, my following you
         on the long journey, my lingering in this shadowy world
under the eaves, out of the storm, where I lie half sleeping
         and half awake, unable to say which way is right
or which is the warp and which is the weft of all such dreaming.
         What matters is knowing that others have gone before:
everything else will be swept away, rusted and eaten till
         only the patterns remain—a stack of punched cards
stored in a museum basement, a pile of dusty boards and lumber
         sold at auction for fifty cents, chopped up and burned
in an iron stove. What matters is that you were coming, father,
         all that way, when I could not see. That you come still.

Changeling

Such, men do changelings call, so changed by faery's theft.

Spenser

Even now I remember them slipping over the sill—
curtains blowing, a light softened by new leaves
and scattering across the ceiling—and I could see
the room in the dresser mirror, from where I lay
in my crib, and know, long before I had guessed
at speech, or where it might take me, that creatures
casting no reflection had come to steal me away.

And only emerged from that trance as a man, grown,
out boating with a friend on a clear river flowing
through a green world, looking down into the water
grazed by our shadow, sensing what passed below—
and hearing him tell how the hunter scans ahead
and beyond the trees, knows in advance what deer
will do, stays in one place until they step forward.

So when my mother went out to the garden, singing
in the light, they were hiding beneath my window,
waiting to take me, and leave another, who was also me,
but changed—as old and fixed in the ways of song
as the hunter who watches, the water that slips by
unceasingly, and is always clear, never the same.
How can I reach those stories now, I who make

no ripple on the stream's surface, and drift instead
toward some wide and lasting place where the water
merges with the sky and the land? Each night I wait
to be changed again, to hear her singing, to know
they have only borrowed me, and are bringing me back,
having taught me to see, through shadow, where each deer
walks in the meadow, and which will be left, which taken.

Mourning Doves

That all my life I have listened to the calls
of mourning doves, have heard them hidden far back
under the eaves, or perched among sycamore branches—
their five still notes sometimes lost in the wind—
and not known how to answer: this I confess,
lying here now, on a summer morning, in a dark room
no less lit by the sound of their soft calling

than by your breathing. And though you might dream
that I lie stretched beside you, I am alone again,
and a child, hearing these same dim voices drifting
high outside my window, explaining to myself how
these are the cries of the newly dead, in the dawn light,
rising toward heaven. Only that, and a child's need
to make up stories on falling asleep, or waking.

And though you might speak, out of that dream, or form
some forbidden word on your lips, my response
would be no more than the music two of them can make—
matching their notes in time, setting up harmonies
that are clear, and pure, and accidental even
to their own reckoning, since all of their singing
is circular, and comes back to the same stillness.

It is back to that place they are calling us now,
and it is out of not knowing that I brush away
strands of hair from your face, and begin to kiss
your eyes, your lips—that I might take sleep
from your mouth into mine, that we might dream invention,
and you hear my confession, and I your answering,
like a song traded back and forth in the morning light.

The Believers

Shakertown at Pleasant Hill, Kentucky.
Winter solstice.

These are the old dreads whispering to me
through the slant light of the meetinghall
this wintry afternoon. Mother Ann Lee
is here, raising a splintery hand to call
for lines to form between the facing walls
and dance the figures that can bring to pass
a momentary clearing of the darkened glass.

A blaze of dying sun brings out the grain
across the wooden floor. Outside this space
their bodies could not touch, nor long remain
together, else some elder's wrinkled face
shone down, from its high watching place,
and shamed them. Here, desire slipped its rein,
the better to be harnessed on a higher plane.

To save by giving what one cannot keep—
mortal to dance, and by such whirling come
into immortal worlds—while others sleep,
to waken from the body's dark mysterium—
these were the steps she taught. And once begun,
there was no turning back, no way to slake
this thirst for otherness except to shake.

And as a tree in winter fills with crows
convened out of some harsh necessity
till every branch is bent and overflows
into a mirroring of what one sees
in summer—creatures become leaves,
all turning, turning in a dark repose—
so did they circle here, and come in close

until they flowered, and it was summer now,
by Shawnee Run, near the stone landing,
where fireflies had filled a sycamore
with single light, and all who saw, standing
along the shore, knew a sure commanding
in that pulse, and walked there, bright
and dark by turns, in the summer night.

None of that charmed singing in the air
above their heads has lasted, nothing remains
of what it meant to dance the hollow square,
to walk the narrow path, the endless chain.
Not even the sun's slow march explains—
here they kept time simply by the swing
of a lead bullet fastened to a string.

The guided tour moves on. I cross the floor
through triangles of light and shade, done
with imagining, yet pausing at the door
to look back on this room, and how the sun
reveals, for just a moment, what will come
when we are finally shaken, and by grace
no longer darkly see, but face to face.

Acknowledgments

Grateful acknowledgment is made to the following publications, in which the poems in this book first appeared, sometimes in earlier versions:

Ascent: "Moiré"
Cumberland Poetry Review: "The Believers," "Changeling"
The Devil's Millhopper: "Mourning Doves"
The Formalist: "After the Rain"
The Harbor Review: "Interview"
Images: "The Purpose of Poetry"
The Kenyon Review: "Seed Storm"
The Laurel Review: "Double Jacquard Coverlet"
The Long Story: "Eidolon"
Midwest Quarterly: "Head of the God of the Number Zero"
Milkweed Quarterly: "For Starr Atkinson, Who Designed Books"
Mississippi Valley Review: "Scryer"
New Letters: "Panorama," "Portrait Studio"
New Virginia Review: "Cicadas"
Oxford Review: "This Is Not a Poem"
Pivot: "Drawing the Antique"
Plains Poetry Journal, "Barn Siding," "Rushlights"
Poetry: "Galleynipper," "For an Old Flame"; copyright © 1987, 1990 by the Modern Poetry Association
Prairie Schooner: "Foundling"
Purdue University Perspective: "Missisinewa Reservoir at Winter Pool"
The Reaper: "The Enchantment," "Frieze," "The Gleaning," "Poem Written on a Line from the *Walam Olum*," "The Shriving"
Seneca Review: "Isinglass"
Sou'wester: "Phoenix"
University of Minnesota Research: "Configuration"
Yarrow: "Cecropia Moth," "The Sprinkle House at Busro Creek"

Several of these poems were reprinted in limited-edition chapbooks: *Fugue State* (Barnwood Press, 1984), *Millennial Harbinger* (Slash & Burn Press, 1986), *The Shriving* (Duende Press, 1990), and *Situation Normal* (Writers' Center Press, 1991).

"The Purpose of Poetry" was chosen for the 1984 edition of the *Anthology of Magazine Verse & Yearbook of American Poetry*. "Mourning Doves" appeared in *45 Contemporary Poets: The Creative Process* (Longman, 1985). "For Starr Atkinson, Who Designed Books," was a Pushcart Prize selection for 1985–86. "This Is Not a Poem" was chosen for the *Annual Survey of American Poetry: 1986* (Roth Publishing). "The Purpose of Poetry" and "The Shriving" were included in *The Music of What Happens* (Orchard Books, 1988).

The author is indebted to the editors of these journals and to these publishers for their generous support. He also expresses his gratitude to the John Simon Guggenheim Memorial Foundation and to the National Endowment for the Arts for grants which gave him time to write many of these poems.